T0113518

WHAT HAPPENS WHEN YOU MAKE
THE WRONG CHOICE?

AKBWH

authorHOUSE®

AuthorHouse™
1663 Liberty Drive
Bloomington, IN 47403
www.authorhouse.com
Phone: 833-262-8899

Published by AuthorHouse 08/14/2020

ISBN: 978-1-7283-6978-5 (sc)
ISBN: 978-1-7283-6977-8 (e)

Print information available on the last page.

Scripture quotations marked KJV are from the Holy Bible, King James Version (Authorized Version). First published in 1611. Quoted from the KJV Classic Reference Bible, Copyright © 1983 by The Zondervan Corporation.

Scripture quotations marked NIV are taken from the Holy Bible, New International Version®. NIV®. Copyright © 1973, 1978, 1984 by International Bible Society. Used by permission of Zondervan. All rights reserved. [Biblica]

Unless otherwise indicated, all scripture quotations are from The Holy Bible, English Standard Version® (ESV®). Copyright ©2001 by Crossway Bibles, a division of Good News Publishers. Used by permission. All rights reserved.

"Scripture taken from the NEW AMERICAN STANDARD BIBLE®, Copyright © 1960,1962,1963,1968,1971,1972,1973,1975,1977 ,1995 by The Lockman Foundation. Used by permission."

Life is reestablished today, however increase is already frozen by prejudice from a history stained by the discrimination of my people. We have a heritage bonded strong by melanin and will-power rooted deep within our veins meant to keep up safe and help us to survive the broken world left behind. The strength of our ancestor's was gifted to us throughout the generations and their tactics to stay strong were kept sacred like a skeleton key to the problems of the world and a brighter future many will fail to see. Our mothers and fathers kept safe the technical, educational, and spiritual lessons we see today in memory books, photo albums, and family legacies created and stored for when the youth are ready to see. We have photos to trace our roots to the very tip of the family tree and obituaries, birth certificates, and newspapers saved to be used like a tool to help level this bumpy road ahead of us, breaking down barriers and accomplishing freedoms not only for ourselves, but our communities.

The children of my generation though are tragically cemented in a state of poverty, discrimination, injustice, and segregation. One hundred and fifty-five years ago slavery was abolished, yet what remains are the same struggles we read about and see in documentaries. When I was growing up, I would witness mothers who struggle and fathers who bail out when things are not easy. Grandparents who work in the lowest tier positions, both underpaid and unappreciated because of the color of their skin. Our people today are kept in those low tier jobs, segregated to low-income living zones, and restricted access to materials of higher education and other necessities we need. Though we protest, it remains silenced, because no matter the statistics, propaganda or political proclamations, our people are hated no matter how many years go by. Therefore, I say protect the young and keep them untainted for as long as you can because they are our future. We need them to continue and keep strong the heritage and traditions of our people; not be converted by the world outside both wicked and cold.

Murder, death, and killing we hear outside our doors; outcries against rape are quieted in the home, and mental illness remains ignored. Many of our monsters are hiding in our own community, yet instead of destroying them, we dim the lights and endure those miseries in silence while others hang their heads in shame as they pass us by. Understand that the difficulties our people refuse to deal with will only fester and grow, eventually seeping through the cracks of the fake smiles we put on so others will not see. Betrayal by our own kin, family lashing out at the unexpecting children like wolves among sheep. How wicked and cruel people are by spreading their own pain and destroying once happy homes; lifelong damage being created and crushing hope. However, every organism on this planet will grow; some disformed and others with deep rooted problems, because like a carbon copy of the environment we are planted in we pick up the same behaviors, mannerisms, and goals.

At a certain age, as a parent you may think you are no longer able to shield your young for their eyes are mature enough to see, minds developed enough to understand, and ears strengthened enough to decipher the language of the streets. No longer can you keep them hidden away inside the bubble of innocence you have created for them and no longer do the nursery rhymes you once sang to stop their cries affect them the same anymore. Your government then pulls your children even further away by developing new laws and policy requiring higher education and independency. Then, as the world outside begins to creep into the rearview; catching up to you before you can get a hold onto the new life developing in front of you, your child is seeing the true colors of society and uncovering the lies meant to keep them protected from the awaiting lion's den they are unknowingly walking into. Look deeper and pay attention, look beyond the glares and cruel slurs and you will see a battle between a system afraid to let us grow and a willful community continuing to push the limit and refuse to give in. So, stay strong and open your minds to better things beyond this life her and now because we are born from people who had a fight in their souls, but not to only survive but to keep their faith in the Lord our Savior, God.

How fortunate I am to have had the grandmother I did; she was a strong black woman full of wisdom and came from a deep south history. Her mind was formed like a cathedral full of well-kept tomes marked with literature, music, religion, and history. From my grandmother I would learn right from wrong, what being a good person really was, and why listening to your elders is truly a virtue when the lessons are so strong. I adopted many of my best traits from her by paying attention to her actions and enthusiastically listening to the stories she told. "Start them young", for me that was the key for I was enrolled in ballet, modeling, piano, IB league schools, and many more activities meant to develop the mind instead of waste away in front of the TV. From day one she would tell me that God put us at the head and not the foot and that she wanted me to lead. Nevertheless, the most important lesson of all that she ever gave me was when she took me to church and introduce me to God. Church service on Sundays, volunteer services on the weekdays, and community vacation bible school in the summer, I would attend them all. My grandmother made sure that if I never learned anything else, I would know the name of the Lord and hold Him high above all. From the Lord's Prayer to Amazing Grace, by the grace of God my grandmother connected my life to the greatest power of all; for He can provide, and he can take away and for most of my childhood all I would know was his mercy, being shielded by his love from the wickedness lurking beyond my four walls.

However, no matter how far we have come, or how prepared we can be with the education of our history there is always a backpedaling situation that will take place. Something always rises out of the dark trying to test our threshold for suffering and our faith for God. In these moments I would recall the odd sayings my grandmother used to tell me. Old words once told to her by her grandmother when she was a little girl, struggling through her pains and her tribulations she had to battle through. One of those sayings I still hold dear and repeat to myself when I need to overcome my fears today and tomorrow. She would tell me that I would see one day when she was old and gone that we do not need the riches, or even the nicest of clothes. She would say, "what we have is good enough and one day because of my struggle, you will have it better than I do". Too young at the time to understand, too ignorant to see that envying what others flaunted did not mean what they had was meant for me nor was having any of those material things what would equals happiness for me and my family. Instead, having a roof over my head, food on the table, clothes on my back; regardless of the brand, and an education is worth so much more than gold. Such things that are now are taken for granted by a generation spoiled by the easy access to resources so scarce in other countries. If only people would realize that the struggles we go through; the 'projects' we live in, do not limit us but make us stronger. I too had to humble myself to this fact, remembering and staying honest to my origins which has only helped me accomplish a brighter future than my history.

From slavery and plantations, to house niggas and segregated water stations that could have been me. Only four generations ago; my grandmother's grandmother life struggle this is my history. Generations of tortured souls reaching through time with letters and photos to teach me that my struggle is nothing when compared to thee. Sally Bentley, born in Mississippi a slave working in cotton fields, only four generations apart, that could have been me. Bound in chains, hung by ropes in trees, my family knows that pain, stories kept and told of the times lived in by Sally Bentley who suffered for our family to be free. So that not by a whip but by my choice I could decide my own future and what I wanted to be. That is the truth of my people I was always told; to keep in my mind and never be without the thought that I can do better and change the world. Because as my grandmother also said, "old 'can't' died in a soda water bottle", meaning there are no impossibilities. As an adult I understand more now than then that it is my duty and not an option to make a difference and change the world. Yet never forgetting those who paved the way for me, because in actuality the only way you can truly make it out of the tribulations you are in is when you create a way for all and not just yourself. Remove the deceptive messages that constantly air on the television screens from your presence, for they preach not of solutions to the problem, but are distractions funded by treacherous intentions and dirty money. Instead make the right your motives and take the hard turns in life. Move forward instead of regressing away from an eternity bright and free. Be the light and shine a light on the path so others may see that just like you and me they too will have better days than what we see today, drowning in this deep dark sea.

I n my adolescence I recall moving around a lot, from a shabby house on fifth and Vine, to an infested duplex on thirty-seventh and Hadley. We have stayed in apartment complexes, duplexes, and rental units we had seen them all and for most of my youth it seemed that we never called a place home for long. That is until we landed at thirty seventh and Lisbon street; there I would spend about ten years of my childhood and go through many situations both bad and good. On the thirty-seventh hundred block of Lisbon street, in the middle of the block and on your left side you will see a white and red duplex with twin porches and a chain link fence in the back. In the late 90's to early 2000's my mother and I would live upstairs and my grandmother a floor below; at the time, I would be starting grade school and my mother would be meeting a new man and soon to be the most impactful person in my life and to my family. Then, at the thirty-fifth hundred block of north avenue, the second to last building on the block would be the brick and mortar that was the home for the fellowship we were soon to be pulled into. There we would be introduced to the pastor and his family, more specifically the son; a declare deacon at the time but soon to be a father figure in my home. This son everyone trusted so much, I would later learn was a drug dealer who along with his sex trafficking brother, were begged to run the family "business". There was strict policy and procedure, and attendance was required multiple times throughout the week. Tithes and offering were collected multiple times per service and although it was pretty hushed the money rarely went towards the church but into the nice cars, clothes, and gold link watches. Looking back through a more experienced lens, the things I saw then were twisted and grim; more like a cult then a church of God is how it felt then. But, what justifications do I have?

This church was very isolated and not just anyone could join the congregation, instead membership was granted by blood ties to the family or marriage into the family tree. The later would be how my family would become intertwined to this self-proclaimed "man of god"; he would present the promise marriage, claiming my mother as his first lady to be. For several years, this engagement would be promised all the while he was closing in and inserting himself into our home. Later would come impregnation and a child that would join my bloodline to his own and as time would proceed this self-decreed prophet would begin to show his truly unstable colors and his demented mentality would destroy my once happy family.

Following this infiltration of the family system my grandmother who was once the head of the home and the wisest person from who our knowledge was learned, no longer had the power or authority. This "man" would obtain to control by isolating and diminishing any protective guidance from our family and friends to keep us under his thumb. My mother's friends would begin to disappear, my godmother, and even family too would be pushed away, and all communication destroyed. Our home that was once full of people, laughter, and harmony now was instead dark and gloomy. Socializing was diminished and if absolutely needed was supervised, if we went out it was with him at her side.

Otherwise my mother would attend work, church, and take me to school; never alone though because as later discovered he always had us watched. Too young, eyes too innocent to understand what I would see, but through it all I knew one thing for sure, that man never loved her. I had seen caring gestures and love from family, friends, and even simple affection from the cartoons I would watch on TV. Instead this man never married and never moved us out of the "hood", we stayed in a struggling situation with danger all around us keeping us prisoners in our own home. We were isolated from family and friends and because of him we were completely alone not even welcome in his own home. Why if you loved us, did we remain in danger why you lived in luxury? You lived in a gated community with open fields to run in, playgrounds, and courts to play on. For even though you had complete control that was not enough for you, you had to make us feel less than and tortured by the want for safety and security that was so close yet held just out of our reach. Family holidays and birthdays, extravagant gifts, and parties, he made sure we saw it all. However, like a child in a toy store, the rules were look but do not touch and when the day was done, you would drop us off like unwanted company to that duplex in the hood with the drug dealers, gangster, and bullets flying over our heads.

Thankfully, no matter the situation and the broken community we lived in, my mother who is the superhero of my life, I was never was hurt, felt unloved, nor wanted for a thing. Kept from my eyes was the wicked ways of man and his cruelties; untainted I would continue to be. Birthdays and holidays whether at home or at Chuck 'e' Cheese would be celebrated. Gifts, both large and small I would receive more than my needs because she would always put my happiness before her own. My security she always ensured, no matter her mental state or the troubling situations, she was there, putting my health before her own. However, one-night when I would older and not so ignorant to certain things, preacher man would slip up; his anger getting the best of him and in front of company. I was not so ignorant to the sounds and grunts, the unwanted touches, and the less controlled facial expressions. That night you were so angry, emotions has been boiling over, you put your hands on her with malicious intent, but this time in front of me instead of the closed doors you favored to hide that monster behind. The pain on my mother's face grabbed my attention, the one who cared and loved me, crying out in pain, my hurting heart bled, and my hands clenched into tight fists. Never again did I want to see that look on her face, neither the pain or freight in her eyes, that was it for me; protection for her I would be as she had been for all my years without fail. He did not like the freedoms she wanted and the care she had for others. Whether charity or friendship, she had such a big heart, but the problem was, he wanted the only place in it.

To this day, I do not understand the possessive nature inside of people that the need to claim another person and control them. The fear that they might lose everything if that person slips away or are without them for more than a second. This was what I saw in this man gripping onto my mother's arm; he would completely lose it and lash out when his insecurities began to show. However, when he hit her, the line was drawn, she was in deep but enough was enough, it was time to go. The fake love did not outweigh the safety of her family and she would decide that far away her family would be from you. So, I no longer stayed isolated in the house nor waited for approval to go to family or friends for the weekend. I was not your child, so to her fullest capabilities she made sure I was free. I spent more time outside of the house, I participated in more after school programs, participated in extracurricular summer activities. As time went by however, you slip back in with promises to be good and you would never hurt her again. She compromised and once again you would come around even though your control over our life was not so strong. Through it all though, one thing she never could control was how thin the walls were, and I could not help but overhear the yelps and muffled screams. Thus, one night when I came shouting, "mom what wrong?" and for me you came raising your hand and that was the final straw. She finally got the picture that a zebra cannot change his stripes and although you may have hurt her, her child you would never harm.

Like a legend throughout time it has been told, how woman become superhuman gaining both super strength and speed to come to the aid of their young when hearing them in need. Stories of woman lifting cars or running as fast as a cheetah when the yelp of their children meets their ear. An internal source of power unable to be replicated and incredibly unique to the female species alone. Too little, too late though when she finally decided it was your time to go, you had already infiltrated the system and a little girl was soon to be born. A little bundle of joy, an actual miracle as the impotency in you was long ago confirmed. But for us she was a blessing and a curse, because although our lives had a wonderful gift on the way, attached was the shadow of your continual intrusions and need to control. Therefore, as we awaited her arrival, we had to accept that for many years you too would remain. So, we stayed put for a while, not quite a stable environment but enough time for the little one to grow. Furthermore, like many male figures in my neighborhood, you were not supportive and only showed up when wanting to see your only child. You did not put food on the table, did not help with bills, nor did you provide your child a safe home. So, for my mother with two children, two fathers only meant two baby daddies, working two jobs, and two mouths to feed with only my grandmother's help to provide and protect the home. Although you were gone from our home, the support system we once had was practically gone; being isolated for so long, going back in her heart felt wrong. But she would keep her word, you would no longer cause us anymore harm or like a whisper in the night we would be gone.

He cooperated, a child of his own made that fury and obsession a little less strong. But only for a short while, because like an addict to inflicting on others your own pain, once again he would come; but what a mistake that was. In a room full of people, confusion on their faces he came bursting into the room, arm raise, and headed in my direction. I would be yelling, "what did I even do wrong?" But no answer would be given, so, once again my mother; my very own guardian angel stood tall, facing your evil intentions, and taking the brunt of it all. Pushing, clawing, screaming, and pleading "don't you hurt my baby" is when the beginning of the end would take place because that night the camel's back had finally broke and the plan was made; flee to another place we would.

The damage was done, my mother's walls were now built

ever so tall. Trust issues, insecurities, and PTSD installed and hard to wipe from her memory drive. We moved again and again, new numbers, new schools, ducking and dodging not only you but your spies too. You came after us with such a drive, your intentions we would never know, and you would never disclose even after all years gone by. Because, you saw your child, of that my mom never denied you, sneaking to find our safe place is something only a coward however would do. So, here we go again with no support and no family or friends to help us through so in silence we would struggle. But if we had each other all would be alright because of the praying and bible lessons, we trusted that God would provide, making up for what we mortals could not do.

To all who read this, learn from my past and know that abuse is never okay, get help for yourself and help those who cannot help themselves. No matter family, friend, or stranger; whether physical or mental, no one has the right to inflict any harm on you. Speak up, get help, run, fight if you must. If you see someone in danger do not stand by because that could have been you. Some people are unable to rise for themselves, regardless of the reasoning it may be. But know that whatever the situation, when you leave, you have self-worth without that person, you are somebody and can accomplish anything. Because, as my grandmother would say, "old 'can't' died in a soda water bottle", meaning there are no impossibilities and you can do anything.

Fast forward about five years and I would be starting high school soon and everything about me would begin to change. No longer was I a "little sunshine", but a tomboy and a rugged teenager. I had to adapt to my surroundings, situations I was in were new, unusual and they felt unstable as once before. Tomboy was a label placed on me because I had begun dressing more in baggy and darker clothes, the other parents said; gone were the pretty pinks and baby dolls. Why, they would ask did I want to be a boy or was a gay like some other girls? At that age I knew nothing of transgenders or homosexual relations, I just knew that I had to be strong in such unsure waters, I had to be stronger physically and mentally, pretty and pink, hair curlers, and girly charms were not the key. What a stronger image than a firefighter, police officer, or an NFL player; typical male figures I had seen on the television day to day. "It's just a faze" and "she will grow out of it" my mother said, but the longer people ignored my changes and the reasons for them, the more I would see that being a tomboy wasn't all I was going to be. I wanted to be one of the guys, playing football and being tough, nothing like most of the girls my age who were playing jump rope or wearing make-up and wanting to be pretty. Having muscles instead of a curvy figure meant I could help around the house by lifting and fixing things like a handyman would do. Being the protector and the fixer of the home was my aim, just like Tim Allen on

Home Improvement who I would use as an image of a good father; a man who would not abandon us again and again.

There was no man around, no fathers, brothers, or even uncles were around to help or protect the family therefore, as the oldest I felt the responsibilities fell onto me. No longer could I worry or dally about pretty things because my family needed me. Being one of the guys however came with a lot more than I was ready to see. The boy talks I would hear, the mannerisms, and habits of a growing teen was not what I needed or sometimes wanted to even see. Because, it is true, teenage boys only think about one thing. Their hormones are racing, their sexual urges are being awakened, however nobody is really controlling or guiding what they see or learn. Thus, comes the discovery of masturbation, dirty magazines, and other pornographic material. But, do not blame the parents alone, because how can parents stop the wondering mind from seeing these things when they are working multiple shifts just to keep food on the table and a roof over our heads. The schools only facilitate the behavior by providing un-monitored access to the internet and allowing kids to roam the hall without supervision, calling it study hall or free periods. Our grandmothers are getting older and cannot quite keep up with the "young ins" anymore, and fathers have all but disappeared, so what better to do for a young curious mind to do than sneak about and getting into grown folks' cookie jars. So, we are flipping to channels on the cable box we know we should not be, stealing dirty magazines, and peeping through keyholes to curve the curiosity. I thank God to this day my grandmother had put the fear of not only God, but the belt and switch into me. Because from so many tempting things that belt would have save me. But how rebellious I still could be, the things on the television and computer screens would create a rebellious teenager out of me. Then, even when my mother tried to correct, eliminate, and teach me the wrongs I had become accustomed to, only much craftier and sneaky I would become.

IV

"**S**piritual slumber", is a state of unawareness and blindness to the distance you have created between yourself and God. I had begun to disregard the lessons and the knowledge I was taught in Sunday bible school, the stories of heaven and hell and all the sinful things a child of God ought not do or I could end up there. For as the bible says in Numbers 14:18 KJV "The Lord is longsuffering, and of great mercy, forgiving iniquity and transgression, and by no means clearing the guilty, visiting the iniquity of the fathers upon the children unto the third and fourth generation." Thus, no matter how forgiving He is, those who choose to sin unresentfully will meet a terrible end. When I was young, I was practically the preacher's daughter, I attended church all day on Sundays, participated in praise and worship and various other activities in the church through the week. Then when I got home, church was waiting for me with family meetings and nightly bible studies. I was never not surrounded by the word of God, I attended multiple Christian orientated schools growing up and in the summertime I would go to vacation bible school with my godmother too. However, as I grew up, I allowed the trickery and vile experimentation of the ungodly things to intrude. Thus, I would begin to sleep, slipping into a dream filled with sinful things instead of the righteous and holy things I should have been pursuing.

Like being in a trance or an out of body experience I could not control myself, only watching myself slip further into sin and deceitful debaucheries. I would seek after these things, but kept my actions hidden from my family because deep down, I knew the things I was doing was wrong and they would judge and ridicule me if only they knew. For the Lord gave us his law, his word infallible and true and from the head to the toe my family were faithful, followed, and passed on the same value they have in Jesus Christ into the generations that followed, which included me as well. Free will but expectation, generations of failures and falling from grace, would that too be me? For once we know of heaven and hell and that God is real, if we choose to disobey and put others before him, forgive us he would not if we do not repent. Then into the everlasting lake of fire we would surely go because without him there is nothing I can do.

Now, through an unforgettable experience, I realize what I was then too blind to see. In my darkest hour I failed to keep my faith and chose to shut the Lord out of my heart and the devil came creeping in. The dragon of damnation and destruction came tempting and twisting my thoughts and beliefs, trying to drag me to him instead. We all had been at St. Joseph's Hospital, my grandmother who had been admitted for a couple of days now was in the ICU and alarms were blaring. She had beaten cancer over seven years ago, she went through chemotherapy, surgeries, and radiation so we thought the battle was won. But little did we know that the cancer had been spreading faster than before and her lungs and brain both were deemed cancerous and her chance of survival was null. An expiration was given and only pain and sorrow on the prescription pad, so at her side in an ICU room we were begging her not to go. Just an hour before I had been by her side talking, laughing, and joking about anything we could, but I was convinced to leave just for a little while. I was told to go take a shower and get something to eat, not to worry because she would be there when I got back; everything would be okay. But when we got back, like a horror film everything was not okay, there was breathing tubes, alarms blaring, screaming, crying, and nurses doing CPR. I had one last look into her eyes, like she held on just to see us once again before she had to go. Then she was gone, my heart broke into two because I knew I would never see that light in her eyes again and my absolute best friend was gone.

I became angry at the world and quietly slipped away from my family, I walked alone to my car, sat in the driver's seat, looked to the sky, and allowed all the pain to hit me that I was holding in. From the bullies at school, the poverty we lived in, my mother's abusive relationships, and my grandmother being gone. The one who always held me when I cried and sang me songs to hush my cries when I was scared and alone. She kept me safe and was my light in this dark world, she gave me all that I held dear, my morals, inspiration, and intuition. "Why Lord, Why?" I would cry out in anger, I would curse and yell and then days later when her own church turned their backs on us and we had to beg family and friends to help bury her, I would abandon my faith because of my shortcomings and sinful deeds that removed me from his grace in my time of need.

With my faith weakened and my connection with God hindered, I would start down a new path of college and adulthood sad and alone. I would travel enter a new area of life with no guidance as my heart was tainted and my head too full to accept that anyone else care since my grandmother was gone. Deep diving on the internet, introduction to drugs and alcohol, almost everything I would experience during this dark time were meant to numb the pain and distract my wandering mind. A few years would blur pass me and I am now a senior in university, I have an on-campus job and a late-night double lifestyle I would tell my mother was just study sessions while I was actually roaming darkened halls. I had more free time, independence, and less guidance over my daily activities. I am however, in a state of confusion about my life's path, my mind is teetering on the fence of being good or bad and the person I want to be, struggles with the image the world sets in front of me. I was not hurting anyone, I was not a rapist or murderer, but would my family approve of my lifestyle choices of extracurricular substances and people entertaining me. But who could I talk to about these questions jumbling around my mind, when growing up in a black family, these topics are not talked about, "it's something our people just don't do!"

Our own shortcomings and dark history we choose not to acknowledge, instead you are shamed and put into a corner if you do; because of this, many of our people are left feeling lost with no identity. Men, women, and children know not where they come from or what they should do, our families for a long time have rejected all topics involving homosexuality, alcoholism, addiction, mental illness, education, and so much more. So much pain our elders went through with slavery and segregation, the problems we complain of now seem so small to the troubles they went through. But now more than ever in a world so lost and cruel, with promotions about the 'fun' things we dare to do. Parents should not be so quick to deny speaking on these subjects because it might pain them to. For if you have suffered enough to give new life, wanting them to be great, and receive the best life has to offer; you must prepare them for all the curves and tricks the world will throw at them.

Reintroduce your children to holy word and bring them back to God. Return to the old ways so that when God does returns, they too can come into eternal paradise through Jesus Christ with you. As I looked around me the I weep for the world, for the churches are less full and some are corrupt or no longer as loud as they had once been. The elders though, through decades and some through a century continue to have faith. The grandparents who have marched in civil rights movements and whose own parents suffered through slavery continue to be obedient to God. Through the hard times and although the seasons change around them from the good to the bad they read the bible and preach his word. But, no longer do the children listen to the old folks as I once did, instead the television and internet consume their minds and fill their heads with the worldly view. Rather than stories of the old times and lesson that could help make them resilient to the tough times, they ignore the wise and instead listen to rap, watch reality shows, and follow blindly to the illusions of fame and fortune than think towards the life after now.

V

At the age of sixteen many young adults are going through a period of self-discovery. At this age many are breaking their first legal barrier of being able to drive and are gaining some independency, a little less parental control on their lives. There is now freedom to go where they please and no longer requiring permission or needing a parental chaperon. Their teenage bodies are maturing, and new relationships are beginning, then you have adulteration in the schools as they are teaching their own theology, morals, and ideologies. College for example, as a level of education most parents desire their children to achieve, is an enormous mental trap. University, underneath all the false propaganda is testing grounds for our faith and a fight for our humanity. During the years of my attendance in university I experienced professors forcing education of manmade historical ideologies, mathematics, science, and biology. No matter if you agree with or believe in what is being taught, in order to gain a degree, you are required to study, test, and practice the theirs truths instead of the ones of God they don't want you to believe.

If there is one thing I had learned, history is written by the winners, meaning anyone can create a story. Whether truthful or what they want people to see. From wars to law or even religion, stories are created by people throughout time that could be made to trick and trap us instead of help which is what college is meant to be. Then at night when the classroom doors close and the dorm halls become alive, a night life vibrates across the campus full of music, drinks, and sex at wild parties. Fraternities and sororities seduce the newcomers and the once innocent freshman are pulled in day one at orientation. The same day the freshman arrive and parents are waving goodbye, their child is swallowed whole by a deceptively corrupt company that profits off of the false hope that a piece of paper will make better the circumstances we are forced to live in. You may question, how a place so many people strive to attend can be so wicked as I make it seem. My truth is that institutions as such; the bigger the worse, objective is to brainwash the young mind. Through testing and practical application required by each student, the young mind is forced to intake so much information in a four-year span that the only thing achieved is a confused, disorientated, and empty shell. They then can fill and form the young mind into what they need to spread their own propaganda and message to corrupt more souls. I experienced as such, when after four years, the certificate I obtained did not change my circumstance but provided me with more knowledge about the world and the image the world wanted me to be.

I implore why these institutions can preach their own propaganda. I mean yes of course; they teach the fundamentals and equations; the black and whites of what knowledge some people may need. Science, math, and biology are all taught and challenge the mind, trying to improve and challenge the standards and break the barriers of the human capabilities. However, the professors and deans also require the study of those extra courses; the 'pre-requisites' of the morals and ethics they want to influence upon you, the theologies of their own propaganda to convert and grab your loyalty. With the extra courses the brainwashing begins, and confusing topics are taught and tested year after year to come. If my faith was strong and my fellowship was fully committed, I may have been spiritually strong enough to resists them, however, like many without faith or yet to come to God, I was not. Thus, not only would this be a dark time for me but also an open season for a claim on my eternal soul and my lost destiny.

After university I would feel accomplished because not many people in my family have come this far, growing up in poverty not a lot of people prioritized a college degree. Now a new chapter was to begin again, the path however was still jagged, rough, and aimed in the wrong direction. Happiness, gratification, and wealth would be my focus, no longer did I care about what others thought or what they would see. The only barrier left holding my complete self-destruction at bay was my mother, because in my heart her disapproval was the only thing that could put an end to my ways. I could not bear for her to ever be upset with me as I had seen so many frowns on her face throughout the years; I would not be the cause for the next. So, as I was hanging on the fence, hovering on the side of degradation, a passion of the flesh is what the bible would reveal to me. "For we ourselves also were sometimes foolish, disobedient, deceived, serving divers lusts and pleasures, living in malice and envy, hateful, and hating one another." (Titus 3:3 ESV) "But if they cannot control themselves, they should marry, for it is better to marry than to burn with passion." (1 Chronicles 7:9 NIV) Deliberately telling me that, the passion, gratification, and happiness I was chasing after would be my downfall, but I did not listen.

Then I was not aware, instead I was fully enveloped in my own pursuit of passion; the pursuit of sex, drugs, and other experiences I had learned about in rap songs or R rated movies. My friends and family's opinion no longer stopped me; however, my actions still went hidden and never spoken of because I did not want anyone to disapprove. I craved the gratification of the dulled senses I found in the bottom of a cup and the approving smiles of the people around me as we dance the night away at some club. Then when the fun would end and I could not find the next fix soon enough again, it felt as if the world would end. I wanted my freedom, passion, the overload of adrenaline, and all the trouble that came with it. I would ponder sometimes if the things I was doing were okay and if letting off some steam and having "fun" was okay since all my hard work was done. I had after all, finished the class work, got my license, and obtained a full-time job, I was even a homeowner now. Why then could not I have this little bit of fun?

I completed my childhood and officially was an adult; all the things people said I had to wait to do until I was older was no longer limited for me. I was responsible all my life, no teenage pregnancy, no std's; I had waited and now it felt like I missed out on so much. Everyone my age had done things already and experimented with things all new to me. Most of them have children now if not two, or three, thus I am just left wondering if I miss something? Was I so focused on what my family wanted me to achieve and not on the me I wanted to be? A mother and a wife, not a nine to five employee trapped working for another person for a percentage not worth it for me. I was left feeling unwanted and unappreciated which was driving me mad, where is my drink?

I as continued lost down the road I was not sure I even wanted to be on, I would begin to sink into a dark place and what would come next to my mind was unfathomable. Thoughts of suicide would creep into my mind, feelings of being unwanted and alone were overbearing and whispering to me ideas of self-harm. If I ended it all now everything would not hurt as much, and the world would hopefully stop taunting me. Yet again when I went looking for help there was none, I was left alone to either end it all or carry on and how scary and unsure those days would be as the beads of blood on my arm did not scare me. My pain tolerance was high enough that if I'd cut too deep, I might not feel it; because what people don't understand is that the physical expression of pain is the only thing that really keeps us from ending it all. Like a built-in defense mechanism your flesh will not let you bite too hard, hold your breath too long, or cut too deep. When I was younger, I would carve into my arms because I convinced myself it would help me feel again. The physical sight of my own blood would prove that I was not fading, or some worthless thing placed here to just work until my body was physically done. I would be taken to see therapists, who only wanted to drug me. The doctors did not want to take the time to understand and what was an hour of talking going to help, when it was years of building issues that I had bundled up inside me. My family did not understand, only saying I was too old for such immature things, everyone had pain and my own was nothing different; just like everyone else in my family there was struggle and pain, therefore I should not take my good circumstances in vain. But as the faithful person my mother was, she would always pray for my health and mental stability. She would ask God to answer the questions she could not and to watch over me when she was unable to, pleading, "please return her home to me".

Now, I am in my mid-twenties, my head is shaven from the locs that had taken so many years to grow and tattoos have been etched into my skin; my arms are filled by dragons and words in languages unknown. My ears, tongue, and nose have been pierced by metal and as radical as you may think, a question I often receive is do I like the pain? My answer is unspoken, but I know the pain is what keeps me sane because if my skin can feel and bleed, I have a reminder that I am still here and my life matters like everyone else. Thus, if I exist, I can change my stars because no fate is written in stone and I can accomplish anything I put my mind to. I had always fear what would come after death, if I ended it all today would there be a heaven or a hell, where would I end up with my life in the state it was? I was not a serial killer or child molester, but I was not an obedient child of God either; I instead was on the fence and unable to commit to one side. Anxiety halted me, fear held me back, and society whispered to me that it was okay to wait. However, I would never renounce my faith that God was real. For even though I was a sinner, my younger years were full of prayer and that faithful foundation anchored me to His feet; I would always be a child of God. Thus, like an olive branch I was given time to question my life choices and deliberate if I would change. Why when I knew what I was doing was wrong, I decided to be disobedient and continue doing wrong. I would question if there could be gay Christians? Can I do drugs and still be a child of God? Do those who commit suicide become angels too? Are all the things I do a sin if I am not hurting anyone? Can I just be a good person, do what I want. and still make it into heaven? Because going to church is a such a burden and people will look at me funny. Bogus excuses would tumble around my mind like sand flowing on a beach. He would listen to each one of my excuses and all my questions, answering each one with words so old and never changing. He would show me where I went wrong and once more I would have to make a choice, but what happens when you make the wrong choice?

VI

struggle with myself because I knew that God had his laws and those that were disobedient I would "go whence I shall not return, even to the land of darkness and the shadow of death." (Job 10:21 KJV) However, since my vision was clouded by the sins of my deeds, I would ignore all I previously learned. I would create many excuses and procrastinate decisive moments regarding my faith and if I would repair it. Instead I continued down the rugged path I was on, not being obedient to the Lord; I listened to rock, fornicated, partied, and played. Something was itching in the back of my mind that my outlets were no better than my struggles, just another thing that would surely shorten my days and I would remain wondering if any of the things I pursue was even worth it anymore. Would my experiences and possessions be worth their weight or would I regret it forever and all my days would taunt me like I had been taunted throughout my life; wanting the things of the world, both silver and gold.

"Ye shall not make any cuttings in your flesh for the dead, nor print any marks upon you: I am the LORD." (Leviticus 19:28 KJV) After I finally "came out" from my dark closet and exposed my lifestyle choices to those closest to me, I am oddly surprise. Just about everyone just accepts my decision to be gay. At the age of twenty-six, the fear of my mother's disapproval was all that had kept my inner desires tucked away. Even when everyone else around me failed to stop me, my family always had a hold on me and if only they knew that releasing me to adulthood was the only thing that would finally destroy me. For, the world is not kind and the people are not good, it is instead a never-ending sea of temptation and suffering. Fun for the wicked is only masochistic depravity and surely if I joined in, Sheol then would be awaiting me.

Nevertheless, the night when I sat at the table and something inside of me told you I had decided, that I maybe liked girls. You cried and pleaded that I did not know what I said and that doing such things were wrong. But my ears were closed and my eyes blinded, what you said I did not understand, like gibberish your words were made because the lures of the world had gotten a hold of me. Like whispers into my ear reasoning and arguments came to my mouth, justification and excuses would flow from me trying to convince not just you but myself as well that my choice was not all that bad. I would exclaim that if I burned for my sin, you would burn with me as well, because all sin is the same and your deeds were no less than mine. Lord forgive me, how could I be so cruel to the one person who loved me unconditionally, that I would condemn from my own mouth so uncaringly. Your past and pain in no way can I perceive, nor should I have spoken on what God has the final say on. Later, I would learn for myself though, through a near death experience leading me back to God, my judge and jury. I would be told my wrong doings and be given the chance to fight for a second chance. A chance to change and grow, with orders to spread the word and knowledge that his word is law; that the final say on all things right and wrong belong to him alone. Both the wicked and the obedient will have a judgement day and that day is soon to come.

I had accomplished all the milestones, and everyone stopped being worried about me. So, like many young adults getting out into the world for the first time without parental controls, we try new things, test the waters, and then dive headfirst straight into trouble. When I was drowning and way in over my head, no one was trying to throw me a life jacket. The focus was on the next generation because I already had my time of being under the wings of protection. I was old enough to know better, but if only my family knew they were never more wrong to stop worrying about if I were one of the good ones and if I would be okay.

As adults we need more guidance now than ever before; when transitioning from a teenager into an adult we are going through a lot of changes, not just physically but mentally as well. We are all gaining new responsibilities and losing many limitations that once held back our uncertainties. At the age of twenty-one the world is wide open as no longer do the age limits hold us back from anything anymore. We can drive, drink, smoke, marry, and indulge in many of the wilder things of which before had always been restricted from us. We are trying to find our new place in the world, trying to establish new relationships, and hopefully create a new family of our own. Becoming an adult can be a scary and an uneasy time in our lives because no one has the answers or keys to make our journey easy. So, trust and believe that even though we are trying to be independent or "grown up" we still need your help and advice.

As parents of new adult's do not be so quick to relinquish all responsibility over your child. We are just as lost as new adults as we were as infants, simply in different situations and new criteria needing to be learned. There should not be an age number on which your child should no longer be looked after or mentored. Leave notes, create handbooks, and tell us your life stories. Take the time as your ancestors did for you to create a toolbox to pass down that we can use to help us level the road ahead that we need to travel through. Understand that the world is a temptress, do not leave us to find our way on our own, because the information available to us today is more dangerous than ever before. Be worried because no longer do the young look to their elders for the answers but their computer screens and the internet, which was once created to connect people; help communication cross mountain tops and desert valleys, now entraps us. Anyone, anywhere, can post just about anything, whether it be video, text, music, or code. All forms of information can be transmitted faster than the speed of sound through our computer screens and become imprinted onto our minds. There have been stories of hypnosis by email and stroke by soundwaves that exist and so does cult conversions by email and obsessive stalker formed by watching videos place on the internet by cynical people. Any question you could ask, can be answered, the only problem is that the answers you receive is not always what you need to see.

The only true guarantee to find the right answer is when we ask the Lord and look to His word. It is written and for those who believe understand that the word is more powerful than any worldly promises or charms. "Wherefore lay apart all filthiness and superfluity of naughtiness, and receive with meekness the engrafted word, which is able to save your souls." (James 1:21 KJV) The Lord has provided us the answers to all things and free of charge, however like all creation we are too curious for our own good. We trust in people we have not seen for information about things they know nothing of. Additionally, that information we allow into our homes then becomes an open the door for the possession of your soul. Though it may seem like harmless entertainment, innocent jokes, or just cool beats to catchy songs, anything you let influence your mind can corrupt your soul. Rap stars promote messages of crime, fornication, and drugs on our radio's stations while producers are airing messages of homosexuality, rebellion, fortune, and fame onto our television screens. All these subliminal and direct messages are then adopted by the young faster than the educational topics taught in their classrooms. Dances, songs, and memes from their favorite social media accounts can be watched, learned, and reiterated within moments, whereas growing numbers of children are unable to read or do simple math. I can admit today that I too had become captivated by these same vices. I watched television shows such as Buffy the Vampire Slayer, YuGiOh, and 90210 growing up. I played video games with rating over my age limit and in high school I listened to rock music, read romantic novels, and snuck into R Rated movies. Thus, as my head was being filled with the knowledge of the world, the word of God I once knew like the back of my hand had begun to fade to the background. I began to doubt the scripture and a new world full of temptation began to tamper with my mind, causing my spiritual being to sink further into slumber.

VII

I now find myself asking how the world has fallen so far from God and why is the enemies work so much louder on the earth in these moments? Advertisements and broadcasts worldwide all are promoting for people to conduct themselves in a sinful manner. Why can't I hear the church just as loudly as I hear the rappers and the reality stars? It is almost as if I do not go searching, fellowshipping, and praying I cannot hear His voice. My entire life I have experienced struggle, but non like this. Even though I am only four generations from slavery, three from freedom rights movements, two from segregated schools, and one from gender inequality, those struggles are null in comparison to my struggle of faith with God. I had stopped trusting God in my darkest hour and my connection was lost, then with world outside became so loud and confusing I would not realize it until too late what I had lost. I stopped attending church, I stopped reading the bible, and when I asked where He was when I needed him the most, the silence would stun me. 2 Corinthians 4:3-4 would explain why, it reads as follows: "But if our gospel be hid, it is hid to them that are lost: In whom the god of this world hath blinded the minds of them which believe not, lest the light of the glorious gospel of Christ, who is the image of God, should shine unto them." I was perishing therefor His voice could not reach my ears, I was already in the dark valley and walking down the alley to Sheol.

Did God not open the skies and make it rain for a

hundred and fifty days when the first of his creation turned away from Him? Did God not smite nations from the lands and oppress them for hundreds of years? Why should I deserve any less for my disobedience, at any moment would I be stricken down too? However, God is an awesome and forgiving God, He is a God of grace and mercy and I praise his name. However, I had to fall before I could understand this. I had to hit the lowest of my lows before he would raise me to my highest. He would have mercy for me even after everything I had done and how grateful I am, but at the same time I remain frightened because now I know the truths, the right and the wrongs, and this would be my last chance to be good. However, the fall I would ever suffer started when I was much younger than I am now. I was in my mid-teens at the time and we had just moved into another duplex, this one not as safe and not as filled with family or good times. We would live on the thirty seventh hundred block of Hadley street and my grandmother would be in an elderly home three blocks down the street. I would be in my freshman year in high school, catching the city bus to a Lutheran school forty-five minutes away in Greendale. My mother officially separated from "preacher man" and now it is just my mother, little sister, and I living in another dangerous neighborhood trying to make it by. From drug dealers to gang bangers, danger surrounds us, yet my mother is still shattered and weak; trying to pull herself together by building up emotional walls that she does not realize keep me out as well. Then when I look around there is no father figure to be found, there is no child support being paid, nor does anyone bother to see if I am alright. So, as the oldest, I would have to step up to the plate; at least I figured until my mother could get it together again. I would be the rock on which my family could count on to hold us above these tumultuous waters.

It started small with just taking out the trash, shoveling the corner, and locking up the house at night. Then before I realized it, I was fixing things around the house and doing the heavy lifting; all the things the 'man of the house' would normally do I took care of now. Random men would bang at the front door, burglars and robber would search for an entry point at the weakest hours. and when they knew that only three little ladies live upstairs at the house on the corner of the block, they double their efforts. However, whether it was drug dealers, rapists, or murderers I did not worry. I got up and I checked the door, calling the cops, and I shouted, "who is it" with bass in my voice. I walked by the curve and I opened the car doors like a man would, my only objective, to make my family safe from the troubles outside those cramped four walls. I would become tough, rugged, and strong for if it was a bodyguard they need me to be for us to get by, for them I would be such for however long they would need.

The more I changed into this tough and rugged person, the more I physically begin to change as well. Tomboy would be the label place upon me as I dressed in baggy clothes, darker colors, graphic t-shirts, and hoodies. I hung with the boys and carried myself as such, gone was the bedazzled flip phones and pretty pinks sundresses and now I played football and video games; I wanted to run with the boys instead of playing with the girls. Why you might ask; why do girls dress like boys, cut their hair, or cover up their feminine curves? We dress "different", so people must think twice when they walk by. They are not so quick to grab, grope, or 'holla' at you when they must question is that a boy or a girl. Men are not so quick to challenge you when you have a my mean look and stocky build; and by me teens I stood 5'8", 300lbs with shoulders like a football player and my hair dreaded to the back. This was enough to cause many to think again before stepping to me, which was exactly what I needed to help me survive the jungle I was growing up in.

When grown men do not provide for their families, they leave their offspring to step up in their place and fill their shoes. Children are taking on the duties of a parent as a placeholder and carrying a title they are not meant to have. The things they then learn and see, not yet ready and too early indeed, causing damage to that child's psyche; but regardless, we do what we must to make sure our family will make it through. We harden and build up walls to protect us, we try to become an ideal man of which we always wanted to be there for us, the perfect family man to make a happy home. Then after so much time spent developing ourselves and doing the jobs you should have; you have the audacity to tell us to dress like a lady and to wear our hair pretty because you raised a girl and not a boy. In response, I say this; and many others would agree too, you did not raise me I grew. Like a flower in the mud I rose to the occasion against all the odds stacked against me and the thicker the mud the harder I had to become, but the harder the struggle to more beautiful the outcome.

Then as time flew by, I would think to myself, why would I want another hard-bodied man to lay beside me? I was already tougher than most of the guys around me, smarter and more mature too. The boys in my age group at the time were both unkind and cruel. The things I saw them do to their own "girlfriends" I would not want them to do that to me too. I did not need another person wanting to control me, take away my self-identity, or physically and verbally abuse me. That would only undo all the hard work and security I had accomplished before them, allowing another person to enjoy the personal qualities about me would only erase my power and self-esteem. Instead I would pursue someone caring and gentle, everything sweet and kind I did not receive growing up from those around me. I wanted some tender, love, and care, but how when everyone I ever met was not nice enough for me to even consider them a close friend. Now I was ready though, I wanted someone to take care of me, love me and hold me. I am ready for a relationship and marriage, someone who is ready to commit and not leave when things become too hard. However, I still do not see that in the men that work around me or live in my neighborhood, these men want to be players and pretend thugs; they want to play the field and be the hottest thing in the yard. In my teens, I attended Milwaukee Public Schools where the boys were fornicating with girls in stair wells and grown men were snatching girls off the bus stops and trading them for liquor and a box of cigs. Then you get older and you see the same things still occurring, sex trafficking of not only girls, but boys, and women too are being abuse, drugged, and traded; so how to I find a man who I can trust when these are the only things I see? On the other hand, your friend who you thought was just a friend, cares for you, is gentle, and protects you. You have each other's back and designated places to meet after school. You start to get a handle on life and learn how to survive better than before because you have a friend who is maybe more than a friend now by your side to hold you down. Your heart starts to beat steady again and the anxiety you carried begins to sting a little less with the assurance that someone is there for you and you will not be abandoned again.

For a long time, right on the cusp of my teenage years I dealt with a lot of mixed emotions, body changes, and my hormones were completely out of control. People were attracted and trying to touch on me that should not have been, the lack of parental control only encouraged strange activities and sneaky rendezvous. My upbringing was unquestionable though, Sundays in church and a stern but fair parent at home, my mother made sure I knew the bible and what entertaining my urges could lead to, however I was enticed by the wilder things the world had to offer at the time. Thus, my days would go by in a blur, I would withdraw inside and close my emotions away in a mental jar. I would continue to cut myself to feel that everything was okay, but none of it really helped. Nevertheless, I had to keep my emotions under control because they would only lead to more problems, people pitying me, and others shaming me. I did not want to disappoint my family by not being the young lady they wanted me to be and not accomplishing the things they wanted for me. Sadly, by hiding those parts of me I only felt more alone and dead inside trying not let out the secret that would destroy my fake bubble of false happiness, peace, and quiet.

My downfall was inevitable though, because being a latchkey kid in the city with terrible after school programs made teenagers curious beings from 3:30pm to 5:00pm.

Getting home after school and realizing you have to house to yourself for an hour or more, watching the programs on TV and playing cans on the block is no longer as entertaining as before. I was told not to leave the front stoop because "stranger danger" was a big deal and having friend over was never going to happen with my mother so paranoid and protective. But the people around me are no better than the strangers outside, reflecting their demons onto me, their pain and troubles affecting me. Trust me when I say that it is not easy growing up in the city. Mothers work double the hours for their family to survive, coming home at sundown only to ask how the day went, before going to bed to wake up the next day and do it all over again. School recitals, basketball games, and award ceremonies mostly go missed and this cut me deep as other parents would be there but not mine. Although she asked, I never told her this because I knew these times were hard. Instead I would retreat to my room and hide my wounds so she would not be disappointed by the things she would surely saw me getting into.

VIII

There is now new life in our home, a new addition to the family tree, and that meant more responsibilities which equaled less attention for me. My problems are now background noise, I internalize them and shut them into a tiny box in my mind. I understand that I had my time and the young need more help than I do right now. I feel invisible and can only hope that someday there will be someone out there for me. I always had this theory that as human beings we are only one part of another half, therefore I must have a soulmate somewhere out there for me. I just must be patient and trust that one day that person will come, because no one is created to be alone. I first began to search for my own soulmate after my mother had told me that she had once found, had, and lost her own. She had met him in high school and immediately they had a once in a lifetime connection; my soulmate must be real too. Till this very day they both still feel a connection just not as s romantic lover would, instead a feeling of care that would never dissipate; because like a person's first love you never forget that once in a lifetime tender, care, and love.

However, many male figures in my community continue to betray their relationship by laying down with another woman. Then they would push the limits of the relationships by having children with this other woman, all while chasing after and pleading their undying love to another. I see constantly in our communities, men committing themselves falsely to a woman and then betraying them by trying to entertain multiple others. Men created webs of lies and false alibis, trying to have their cake and eat it too. Women in response build up walls to guard their hearts and their children see and repeat, becoming untrusting of men and deeming them unworthy before they can get close enough to hurt their family again. But not only do men cheat, domestic abuse rates are so high, people are more scared to stay at home than being out in the streets. When did the development of the human brain go so wrong, that insecurities, jealousy, and obsession developed to such a cruel degree?

There would be a total of five men that I would see come and go in my mother's life, all of them potential a father-in-law trying to court my mother but never being a good fit. Some were abusive and others were filled with jealousy to the point that their own insecurities destroyed the relationship before it could even begin. There would be ultimatums given that my mother needed to choose between her kids or him. Then came the verbal and physical abuse over wages, household necessities, selfish gains. One relationship after the other would take her energy and tamper with her faith that there was ever anything good in a man she would ever meet again. But, what does my mother's relationships have to do with my relationships and why behave in the manner I do?

When women have relationship in front of their children, that relationship includes that child as well; we watch, listen, and learn from what you do. From the talks on the phone, to the facial expressions you think go hidden but we see. Good or bad, we see it all and your failures we try to avoid and your happy moments we remember and hope to someday achieve. It is not that all the failed relationships I would see made me the way that I am and have thoughts of homosexuality. Neither would the cutting of my arms or the mental struggles I had be the fault of the abuse my family members went through. My behavior was not as the shrinks would say, a cause of "mommy daddy issues" or a lack of a "father figure" being there. Every man that courted my mom had potential to be stepdad of the year, but instead they wanted to do their dirt and have things their own way. But not only in the home, I saw this behavior everywhere, at school the boys would talk dirt about the girls and trade them around like playing cards, on the city bus, you saw women mistreated and heard stories about little girls getting abducted for being too cute. In my home, not just my mother dealt with difficult relationship, but many other women in my family dealt with issues of abuse, betrayal, abandonment issues, and rape. Women were seen a weak and something to play with by the men I saw around me, I decided I would not be taken advantage of next.

Inside my heart there has always been an inclination to protect others, to be the lion and the bear, to stand tall and roar, for when others could not fight for themselves I would. Being a protector was never asked of me neither was I groomed to do any of these things. Instead I was taught piano and ballet as a child, I was dressed in pretty pinks and kept oblivious to the hardships of my family's for as long as they could. On my own I would pick up on the tension, the worries, and the doubts. I realized that no one was there for us and then I would decide to fight, I decided I could be a defense when in need and a provider when others would fall short. So a new path would open before me, but instead of doing wrong I'd choose to pursue an education and create a way out of the hood, taking my family with me my only priority; for when the men could not I would.

Four years of university to achieve a bachelor's degree with aspirations that one day I would be somebody. Living off campus meant driving to school in the early morning hours and cautiously walking to my car at night, because downtown was notoriously dangerous and campus students were constantly getting mugged for their cell phones, laptops, and even campus issued textbooks. Nevertheless, I would keep my head down and get a campus job which made my nights even longer. But an additional source of income meant my school needs were one less bill and would keep me on my feet. I would tough it out at minimum wage because as a colored person we do what we must first, so that later we can do what we want. So, I flipped burgers in the dining halls and worked at the bookstore in the summer; all while carrying a full load of classes, day to night I worked hard to get my four-year degree.

University was nothing short of a challenge though, unbeknownst to me of more than just my mindset was being tested, but my spiritual capacity as well. Regardless, continued to push the limits, determined to finish school, and persevere against all the odds stacked against me. I purchased my own car and got another part time job, I took care of more than myself but also the home with a bag a groceries here and there and a couple dollars stuffed in my mother's purse so times were not so hard. Then, at night after all the work was done, along came some college campus fun. About junior year finally it all was going good and we finally were making it out the hood, slowly but surely from Lisbon to Hadley, then Villard to Oklahoma there was steady paychecks and food on the table, we did not worry when the next tragedy would strike or if there was a drug dealer at the door. Everything was finally going well, however like a skipping record to the story of my life, when things are going good something always must go bad.

University graduate, four-year degree, and a summer elective program; what career field did you think a black female from the inner city would go into? Decades have gone by and still my people are misled, we are steered into dead end careers unknowingly every day by guidance counselors with wretched agendas to keep us out of their neighborhoods and back on the streets. Much like in the 60's, segregation today is slight but sure; Teachers, universities, and governments have motives to keep our people in low tier positions and confined in terrible conditions. We are paid wages that leave us unable to afford to move forward and impossible to live in better communities. They attack us not with dogs, hoses, or their batons but with limitations and policy to further their own goals.

Our people, just as I find myself today are financially, intellectually, and physically trapped. Like an elephant in quicksand, we are reaching out for help only to receive the short end of societies special programs designed for reverse progression, debt, and dependency. Large quantities of people are living paycheck to paycheck with unaffordable bills for water, heat, and food. Because of societies standards they leave us to struggle and fight for the scraps and instead of providing us with a better education system and higher paying jobs, we are given food stamps, welfare, and low-income housing programs. However, much like our ancestors who worked the cotton fields, back was flayed open by whips, and legs were chained, we survive. But survival sometimes is not enough, this cannot be all there is in life, struggling to survive the hatred of others undeservingly placed on me.

First were the boats stealing our people away from the homeland, then followed slavery, civil rights movements, and segregation. Even to this day our people are hated, gun downed, imprisoned, and treated as less than. When I look deeper into the situations and circumstances our people are made to endure, I am reminded of the Israelites and their disobedience to God. Because of their behavior, they were meant to suffer hundreds of years as Acts 7:6 KJV reads; "And God spake on this wise, That his seed should sojourn in a strange land; and that they should bring them into bondage, and entreat them evil four hundred years." Has history repeat itself again, are we the Israelites and this is our generation's four hundred years in a foreign land?

My career is a dead end, walking the isles of a dark locked room with seventy grown men on bunk beds who could potentially fatally harm me was not how I imagined my life journey's end. These men are at their worst and act much worse. They are angry, aggressive, and in utter despair and this is not a way I ever want to see my people again. Grown men fighting over food, bathing in what can only be described as a ditch in a dark room. The mentally disabled are isolated and ignored and the drug addicts are handed more pills to hush their groans of withdrawal. Homeless who unfortunately become entangled in the law, are expected to adjust or risk physical retaliation and weeks in segregation dormitories. The cruel things I saw would only further confirm that the system is corrupt beyond measure and cares nothing about the people at the bottom, whether innocent or guilty: it is dog eat dog out here

So how do I find my balance, find my happiness if you would say? I would decide that sexual gratification would be my vice, my escape from the long shifts and the nonstop bills. However, not being interested in men and instead the fairer gender, I knew I could not have any real relationship or ever bring a woman back home to me my mom. If I ever did, I knew that would be the final nerve that would break my mother's heart. So behind closed doors I would do my deeds, but never a relationship and never anything real. I am grown but cannot do grown people things because it is her house I live in and her rules I had to live by. You do not complain, argue, or talk back; you do as your told because the rod spoiled the child was the law of the land in my mother's home. So, I internalized my emotions, even as mixed and jumbled as they are, all of it building up about to explode. Of course, I could have moved out, but a lot of people who leave home never calculate that move before they do. Rent alone is your first paycheck of the month, utilities, internet, and food just add on creating a deep hole of debt unless you decide to get a second job. Then not to mention the unsafe conditions of living alone, especially if you live in the hood because the rent in the suburbs are unaffordable for someone of my color. So, my options were to stay at home and help with the bills so I know neither one of us would have to struggle and be in danger or selfishly leave so I could do my deeds. My heart just wouldn't let me make that decision, but like sitting on a teeter totter on a playground, I would play a game of up and downs, trying to balance between following the rules and having some adulterated fun.

To you all, I give words of advice; gain independence and obtain skills of self-care and provision. Because dependency on others to provide for you will only kill your spirit and hide your true potential. Whether it is family you depend on for finances or the government, make a change and achieve something for yourself that no one else can place a claim on. Depending on others to always come to your aid can be a deep, dark hole of disappointment that will lead to depression and anger. Finish school, get a job, create a business of your own, gain the ability to take care of yourself, because in the end, when reckoning day comes all you will have is yourself to count on. No one can save you from the life you have lived and the choices you made throughout it. However, understand that independency does not mean you have to be out alone. You do not necessarily have to leave the nest and fly on your own to be an adult, historically many families would have multiple generations living under the same roof, all helping to provide and working together so that the burden did not fall on one person alone to carry. Not everyone is financially able or spiritually meant to live alone, they are stronger together and are able to understand the boundaries needed to allow everyone to grow. Never forget where you come from or the people who struggled to help you get there. Others have given up their dreams to give you the chance to grow, when you fly high do not forget to bring along those who cleared the sky for you to soar.

Present day, I am a homeowner, a full-time employee, and finally in a good place it seems. My youngest sister moved away to live with her father but visits on the holidays, but no longer do we worry so much about her as she has gotten herself together and is a soon to be high school graduate now. We are financially stable enough for my mother to go back and complete her degree too; she had put everything on hold when my sister and I were born, so now that we are grown, it is her turn to achieve her dreams. We have also found a new place to call home, it is not a mansion but extravagant has never been our style. Work is going good, mom's health is doing better, thus life is no longer as heavy on my chest and finally I feel like I can finally breathe easy. The only thing missing though is the mate to my soul, that one link is still missing in the chain to my happy ending.

So, I finally explode, "I think I might like girls!" What the heck was that? I glance at my mother's face and for the first time in my life I see utter disappointment and then the tears come. I must still my heart because out of everyone in my life she is the only one I never wanted to be sad because of something I had done. Born one day and twenty years apart, my mother has been my closest friend, my confidant, and my safe place. She is the only person on this earth whose happiness would always come before my own and whose approval I continue to seek even though I am grown. But something inside me is headstrong in my decision that at twenty-six years on this earth my happiness would outweigh it all. Then I hear the words "it's okay, I love you", she says my choices are against God and are not okay, but that no matter my wrong doings she would always love me. And even though I am not completely sure of this choice I made, I can breathe easier with my worries that anything I could ever do or think would destroy my families love for me. Being so withholding and emotionally closed, I just wanted to be myself and to be accepted as such. The little girl inside that never got to grow or live, that needed tender, love, and care sparked back to life by the warm flame of your words.

To my family and friends, thank you for accepting me. In my darkest hour, when I failed God you would not fail me, and that type of unconditional love would bring me back to reality. Additionally, to those out there who may have thoughts about suicide or even have attempted self-harm, know that you are not alone. We all will go through hardships but fight through the pain because it will make you stronger and more resilient than those who have it easy. It is okay to be different, not to have it all, and to have to work for things others are just given. Do not take it out on yourself, I have been there and have scars mentally and physically to prove that some situations will get the better of us. Therapists, help groups, hotline, and many more resources are in place to help, you do not have to go through your pain alone. Understand that God will put us in situations that will challenge us, sometimes those situations may seem too hard to bear, however he has a purpose for all that he does and He will never give us more than we can bare.

Pushing through my own ordeals I have become more

resilient to the cruelties to world holds instore and I can make decisions for myself I struggled to make before. Sometimes, I wish I was still a child though without all these new responsibilities, no more paying any bills, working a 9-5 job, and all the other things I now know are over-rated when I just could not wait until I was twenty-one as a child. Nevertheless, I am continuing my journey to finding myself again, I have realized that what I have is meant for me and that with effort and God's grace I will be given what He has instore for me. To you I say, do the same, look forward and have faith, aspirations, and continue to dream. Because when you have something to work towards, you put a purpose on your life to keep move on. It is okay to feel emotions, whether it be happy, sad, glad, or mad but you must get up and move on. Push through and search for something more and your vision for your life will become clear again. Yes, there will be doubts and there will be pain too, but do not let it hinder you and what one day you will be able to do. Get out there, join a ministry group, make a business plan, or even go back to school; but make sure you keep your eyes sharp. Do not be blind to the temptations of the world, because there are tricks and traps that will be set you before you by the enemy to distract you. Some days you may not want to wake up and deal with the world anymore but try to find something or someone that will make your days bright again. Adopt a pet, but a plant, or make a new friend because the little things we take for granted and disregard will be the very things that can jumpstart your life again.

IX

March 7th, 2020, I think I died. I awoke to darkness with no body and on no physical plane. The Lord came and told me I died and how, that I was gone and not to a good place as I hoped. I thought it was all over in that moment, the pain and the message stunning me till this day, but he gave me one last chance; He saw me going down the wrong path and sent his angels to show me His way. But those angels would also show me the way of damnation that I was taking if I continued to live the way I do. Twenty-seven years young, still an infant when compared to his vision for me. Living in world of good and evil, and given the gift of freedom to choose my own path, yet with that gift was also a curse as by our choices we make, we will also be judged. The Lord is all mighty and all knowing, all seeing and all powerful; every person created by His will must fall into place underneath him as such. Therefore, when I thought my deeds went unseen how foolish I was, what though about, dreamed of, and acted on was all seen and marked against me and on March 7th, 2020 I would meet my maker and be judged by my jury.

"Grandma Earnestine!" is what I would scream, begging for her to save me from the pain that was brought upon me. I threw my head back, kicked my legs, and beat my fist; I was somewhere I should not have been and was fighting for whatever was causing this pain to end. I was told time and time again to stay away from there and to stay out of grown folks' business, however I did not listen. Does everyone have this one last experience? Do people choose to ignore the warnings and say He is not real after experiencing something like this? Well this night was enough for me, some days I still feel the pain of that like little reminders of his wrath bestowed upon me for my sins. Pain would radiate through my body like a live wire, the shock would travel up through my feet to my head and down through my abdomen enveloping me. All those warnings my grandmother had told me, but I choose to ignore, I wish now I would have listened; how much better off I would be than in the predicament I am in now. She taught me to be a leader and not be a follower, pleading that I would have the strength to withstand the evil and trust in God. She would tell me to fear the Lord in all things because He is the provider for all things but also the taker; thus, with my life on the line I wished I would have listened because from me He was ready to take everything.

Choosing to do the wrong thing, going against His law when I once knew it so well would hurt me though because the knowledge that because of my choices, I would feel that pain for all eternity and just being obedient could have prevented it all is a pain so deep it words alone cannot explain it all. Excruciating, mind numbing, galaxy ending, both white hot and black cold pain all at once was exploding inside of me. Every limb, bone, and nerve knew nothing but pain, there was no escaping my fate, not even to God. To find relief I would try to reach for Him and grab a hold, praying he would not let me go. But only those who followed his laws and kept his commandments, read, and practice his word would be kept from this pain. So many times, He has told us not to do the things we do; he even shows us what we are going to do and when we will do it; still we ignore Him and choose to sin and that he will not forgive. But one thing people fail to understand about God, through his wrath and the all-powerful being that He is; we are all children of God and He wants above all else for us all to make it to heaven to live in him forever. "But the God of all grace, who hath called us unto his eternal glory by Christ Jesus, after that ye have suffered a while, make you perfect, stablish, strengthen, settle you. To him be glory and dominion for ever and ever. Amen." (1 Peter 5:10-11 KJV) So why do we ignore and choose the temporary things instead? They will all fade and fail us in the end.

The songs we sing today in the churches have been sung throughout time and the very same songs sang on the plantations not so long ago. Four generations from my life, my grandmother's grandmother a slave. Through their turmoil they would raise every voice and sing the songs of praise and worship to the Lord and it would keep them strong, their mind and body whole. God appoints his angels and satan assigns his demons, both able to enter our world and test the faith of our souls. Thus, free will comes as both a gift and a curse, for the Lord even with all his power will not choose our fate for us. The choice of everlasting grace or damnation he leaves to us alone. Generations upon generations ago God's creation would choose to betray and disrupt the natural order He had in store for us. Before these times we suffer now, God himself would appear before us in smoke and thunder answering our prayers in person, performing miracles, and destroying our enemies. Now however, we doubt Him by asking if He is real and why He allows the tragedies and disasters to fall upon our world?

The first ever to make the wrong choice was Adam and Eve, the first to be told the consequences and the law and to be corrupted by the desires of their flesh to instead of listening to the Lord, choose their flesh. However not only for themselves did they choose, but for us as well, as we are their children and we all come from that garden of Eden; from the womb of Eve, birthed through pain and suffering. Then because of the eating of the forbidden fruit from the Tree of life, God created and trusted in the presence of man. The forbidden fruit of the flesh, the same I longed for, feeling and affection from people He put into my life. My last option to make that night would be revealed to me, pleasure and pain or his mercy and grace. My choice would not be easy, the experience and path unsure and unpleasant. But here I am now, my choice, my last chance. Had I been so far off the track? Teetering on the fence so soon on my journey; so near to betraying the law and doing the unforgivable.

In my mind I had wanted one thing, but we all know that the pain we were warned about by our mother's; His bride, the one who is our gift of his mercy, comfort, and care, that could save us from damnation, but only if we obey and choose him above the temptations of the world. But someday they must let us go, when we're old enough and tell them we understand but still want to do wrong, that even though they taught us and tried to save us from the foretold suffering we would endure. Pain so unfathomable and exhausting to the point that the pain you thought you would feel is nothing compared to the pain you would feel in the end. And when you give up fighting against the pain, it finally hits you that you had been told and choose to ignore it, the grace of God you would not make it into because of your disobedience to all the things you were already told would come for you. God created you and wants to give you another chance to save yourself, to correct your ways, and to live in the way of the Lord; to achieve your destined purpose he has instore for you for it has already been told. My destiny is to help others like myself, who are growing up in a world of cruelty, betrayal, and despair. Where growing up at 1939 N. 37th St. and peeking under the blinds at the bottom of the stairs and a world of gangsters, drug dealers, and murderers were all I could see.

The scene changes, the drugs are no longer on the streets but in a bag on the floor. A man is yelling at my mother as tears are streaming down her face. I look around and see girls shaking their butts on the TV, young boys robbing, girls doping, and selling their souls; children with no guidance, without a "Grandma Earnestine" I had to protect me. A grandma who shielded me, kept me safe from the evils awaiting me beyond that slowly creaking door, because when you are alone that is when he will come, but my angel from above surely was sent down to cover and guide my precious soul.

My mother was indeed the giver of my life, from whose womb I was delivered and nurse to health, being raised up good and strong throughout the burdens and struggles of her own. However, my grandmother has always been my keeper and I am sure just as I have now, my grandmother and mother both had met their day of decision and had to make a choice to follow God or fall as well. They both must have been shown their last chance because the temptations of flesh are strong within us all and no one is perfect, least of all the family in which I have grown. Paternally I see gangsters, dealers, and fornicators; maternally I see drug addictions, rapist, and criminality. There was family I was not to be around alone because they could not be trusted. Cousins that might influence the bad, the good not always done by them behind and outside of closed doors.

Much like a B and B my childhood home would see many faces come and go, strangers young and old, family like snakes and untrustworthy young and old. But this was how they survived their own battles; pain was drowned in a bottle of crown royal or dulled by the needle with something brown condensed down. They probably all were shown their last chance to do right, because the temptation of the flesh is surly strong within us all and no one is perfect, neither is anyone capable of being unaffected by the things they'd see growing up in the streets of humanity. However, whether right or wrong, a decision must be made; shall we listen to the serpents in our lives or believe in His word, both infallible and true. The bible tells of the beginnings and the ends, the struggles of those who came before us, and the very same temptations and decisions the people within were tempted by back then. People who made decisions that affect us all and as such we are to be judge and weighed by our actions and decisions as well, for it is told.

If only I had listened before, but what would life be without free will to do wrong or right, no challenges, no mystery, no wonders, or excitement without the maybes and what might be. Would we really be living and not just action figures for Him to play with like chess pieces on a game board. No failures or success, we would neither grow nor transcend for we surely were created for more than just this. I remember now as clear as then, when someone said that "we are spiritual beings having a human being experience", that we were sent down to experience life and to learn. But will we pass the tests and tribulations, will we make it back to His glory? A lot about our existence is a mystery and for many people there remains this aching need to always know why and to have all the answers. That curiosity and untrustworthy aspect within us though, is the very things that condemns our souls.

Many people have trouble just accepting their lives and being grateful with what is given instead wanting more; seeing others with things given to them and sowing jealously and rage because they were not given these things too. But as the word says, He will not give us more than we can handle and not to store up treasures in a temporary place. Money, clothes, riches, and gold has no meaning or value on our souls, our focus is placed in the wrong areas by people so concern about their own existence but not going to the literature of the holy word. Nevertheless, my trial would commence, He would reveal to me, unto my utter astonishment, my wrongs, my wonders, and my destiny. The one thing so many people struggle to figure out; their purpose on earth and why they were created, God would willingly show me and all I could say is, "my God".

Greek letters, much like the Alpha Zeta and Omega the Fraternity and Sororities wear on a white tee. Family there with me and together we stand in unity to fulfill the plan; complete our destiny. I wonder do they know, has God told them too, how will it happen, and how do I get there? After the ordeal of that night, which I will explain all in full detail, I remain in pain, body and mind fuzzy, trying to think and pull myself together, and scared out of my mind because with my ripped clothes, location, and heart monitor on my smart watch not giving life signs that night, there is no doubt in my mind that it was all real. I cut everything out cold turkey, everything must change now, if it is ungodly it must go. Determined to know all of God's law again, front to back I will read the bible again, I can make no mistake of being ignorant; no excuses He told me that night so going forward I'll be sure of the things I do. Now that I have had my experience, an after death or out of body some might call it, everything makes since now. No longer spiritually do I slumber, it's almost like an alarm clock was going off all this time and I had been ignoring it, sleeping through it with glee unaware that this was the one alarm I did not want to miss because if I wait too late there would be no forgiveness and I would wake up in a place I did not want to be.

But, why do people choose the pleasures of the flesh when the greatest gift of all is already promised to us. He loves us and will provide all we need, there is nothing we should want that would jeopardize or challenge His love and grace of us. You are not able to serve two gods', nor are you meant to worry over the worldly things, instead we are meant to love thy neighbors and be His sheep; obeying the Lord our Shepard in Jesus Christ, our savior. Additionally, just as he had given Adam, he too will give us all the missing pieces; He will provide what is not to be looked for or lusted after, he will give us one whom will walk through this world with us. We are not meant to be alone, but we are meant to be patient, most fail to understand that patience is the master key. People also fail to realize that a soulmate is not just a lover, but a soulmate can be a friend, a parent, or a stranger you have yet to meet. The relationship does not have to be romantic in nature but can be of a guiding nature or the greatest friendship you will ever have on earth. Yet our free will allows us to make a lot of wrong choices in our lives, how we go about living our lives, and how long they will last. No one has control over you, and no one can save you in the end, but anyone can impress upon you either steering you right or wrong.

Help the young see, bring the programming like I had when I was a baby, show them the truths of good and bad, reveal the consequences beyond death that awaits them for they know not what true pain feels like, nor what temporary pleasure leads them to. The Lord wants for us all to come back to him, and if only someone could grab and shake them, scream on the mountain tops, and make them understand that they have gone too far. The things people chase after matter not, they do not build up your mansions in heaven nor put your name in the book of life. Clothes, shoes, money, hair, nor where your live will add a morsel to your worthiness to God and there will not be pity or mercy, as the suffering have now is null when all you had to do was have faith in God. "Therefore I say unto you, take no thought for your life, what ye shall eat, or what ye shall drink; nor yet for your body, what ye shall put on. Is not the life more than meat, and the body than raiment?" (Matthew 6:25 KJV)

X

I could hear my nana in the other room, time rewinding to my earlier years before my very eyes. I had to be maybe two or three years old, my very own angel whom I had lost was going to walk through that very door, and she was the only thing that could stop the tears and still my sorrows. That night I was with two other angels of mine, family that were once so close before that overtime I had fell out of contact with but still had a bond so strong. March 7th, 2020 to serve as a testament to others, to the youth growing up in the same streets I once had; those children who may be teetering the line as I was and may be near the end of the line close to their final chance. My night, the experience of heaven or hell that I now tell hoping to wake others up and show them that God is real and that through repentance he will forgive you as well.

That night began at the movie theater, I was going to see a new movie, a remake about an invisible man from the 90's. This night was my chance to get my hands on some edible I had been bugging to get for an entire month now. For a while now I had been on a kind of bender involving partying, drinking, and other recreational drugs. For weeks I had not been acting like myself, what I would say was simple "fun" would involve unsure experiments in dark rooms with people I would say were friends but really strangers to my true needs. So, when I finally got to the theatre, I would eat half of my edible and prepare myself for more "fun", then halfway through the film I decide I am not feeling it and have another piece. Of course, they both told me not to and to take it slow but as hard-headed and strong as I think I am I made up my mind that a little THC brownie could not affect me. "Big dog is not feeling it" I say, speaking a little too soon as like a slow-motion special effect everything slows down, and I am now strapped onto a ride I no longer want to be on. I need to concentrate just to walk down the theatre stairs after the movie is over, holding on to the person in front of me to get back to the car without looking too much like the idiot I know feel like. As I sit down in the passenger's seat, I sigh with relief thinking I am safe and just get me home and I will be okay. But, oh boy was the ride going to be a long one and the hardest fight of my life was ahead of me.

They are laughing at me and my antics as I begin to hallucinate and spaz out at the things I feel and see. I am not able to recall everything that night during the drive, what I must have done in the car to this day is like a blank space in my mind and thankfully the memories are gone. Part of why I started experimenting with alcohol and drugs though was because it would remove my inhibitions and self-control, I felt it made me courageous to do and say things my usually reserved self never would. Like liquid courage, I thought taking these substances would help me be more outgoing and fun, but this was a lie I had been telling myself, so entranced by the actors on TV hoping that if I tried what they did I would have some fun. However, I later had to learn that when putting oneself out there, the worst that can happen is to be denied or rejected. However, until we try and fail, we will never be able to try and succeed. There is no need for drugs, alcohol, and fake friends to cheer you on, no need for the approval of others because all this life is temporary; the little fun experienced now is nothing in comparison to the wonders of the eternal life to come.

"You don't really live until you die", my youngest sibling would tell me, I did not fully understand her at first, but now I realize that the life we live in this place would not be the end. Why then should we long for passion and satisfaction of the flesh, being tricked by the fictitious needs of the human mind. Faith and obedience should be the focus of our life, to do as God commands of us, so that we may be chosen to dwell in his presence and look upon his face.

They are telling me to drink some water from the bottle in the cupholder, as if it will help dull the effect of the drugs in my system that now torment me. What a huge mistake as my body now feels like everything in it is alive and moving without me. My organs, nerves, blood, and now this small amount of water are crashing side to side like tidal waves within me. They continue to laugh as I struggle and freak out even more trying to stop waves from coming into shore. I think I can slow the wave if only I can sit completely still and calm, but then somebody swerves the freaking car making the waves more violent than before. Regret, pain, and paranoia now fill my thoughts I remember something she said that happen when she ate this edible before, what did she say happened? Oh yeah! She had a body malfunction, oh no, is that what is going to happen to me? So now I am just trying to concentrate and hoping this terrible ride ends soon.

We arrive at their house, a childhood favorite place to go, filled with memories of family and fun. Somehow, we make it up the front stair to the door and it is like I am a toddler again. The bottom of the stairs still has the shovel by the door we played with when we were young and then realization strikes me, like a little kid riding in the back seat to the park or a store, I figure out where we are going and become over joyed. "I loved going over here and I always had fun", I would think to myself. I try to get up the stairs a bit quicker now and I cannot believe my eyes, I see our shoes outside the living room door we wore when we were little kids a time and a half ago. Little kids' tennis shoes and grown up church shoes that could not really be there now because that lady moved away and her kids are much older now. I turned and ask them is its real and if they see it too, they smile saying yes and to keep going, that there is more beyond the door. Oh my Gosh! This edible is amazing I now think, I have time traveled to the past, I was walking in the same living room as I did in the 90's, there was the same pillows on the couch I had use to make forts and the same pictures on the mantel with family some gone and passed away since then. I walk further into the dining room and I stop asking" where's the computer?" The one we played Leap Frog and Oregon's Trail on was gone, "where's the computer" again I say; the lady always took the computer away when they were in trouble, and with no computer we had to do something boring all day long. They both looked at me and laughed telling me to keep going and that there was more beyond the door. I keep walking into the kitchen, I see the red microwave and the round kitchen table, I even see the room in the back corner, full of posters, dressers, and the bed linen from before. Then I turn and go into the master room and I hear something and turn back around, a voice is coming from the other room. I head down the hallway past the bathroom towards what I remember to be my favorite room to play in back then. I do not see the bunk bed or the dresser and posters of a kid's room though; I see my mom's old room; one I was too young at the time to remember the address of. And there she is, so much younger, but my mom all the same sitting on the bed talking on the phone. I look around and recognize everything from pictures to the bed spread, everything is so vivid and real. I begin to cry because I am starting to remember something else about this room, and I hear someone else in the background calling my name. It cannot be! I love her so much, it cannot be her, am I going to get to see my nana again.

I become even younger, regressing in age and stature, it cannot be her, is she here, I ask my them now standing afar. They smile and nod, much like before. I am crying harder now, on my hands and knees, pleading and peeping around the corner of the bed, "nana!" Is it her? Someone is getting closer, I can hear the footsteps and most of all I can hear her voice, I think she is calling my name. But now I am wailing, "nana Earnestine!" "nana Earnestine!" My words however are becoming less distinctive as she is getting closer to the door. Then like being pulled away, I am out of my body looking on from above I see a child that must be me throwing tiny fists and feet around; throwing a fit on the bedroom floor, screaming for nana to come save me from whatever must've made little me upset shortly before. Then like a sweet melody, I hear my nana say, "shh, nana's here everything is going to be alright".

The scene stops and my shins being to burn with an increasing ache and then a burst of pain explodes within me and everything goes blank, I wake to nothing but darkness and a withering silence in the air. I feel like I am waking up, but I cannot see, nor with time does this change and my mind begins to race with possibilities and the worst thoughts of what may have happen to me. As my pulse begins to race and I begin to panic, I hear a voice in the darkness telling me to take deep breaths. "Breathe in, breathe out" the voice says, repeating the instructions repeatedly. There is no movie, nor novel that can prepare someone for this moment; there is no uploading to a cloud neither an awareness nor control over what is going to be, the next words I hear are "you have died". Where, what, when, and how? So many questions come to mind, so there is something after death, but then one stuttering thought comes to the forefront, where did I go, heaven or hell?

I am taken back to my mom's old room; I see myself throwing a fit on the ground and the scene begins to unfold. My shins are on fire because I am scraping them on the bedpost at the edge of the bed, my mother is trying to console me, and I am screaming for nana to save me. I had done something I should not had; toddler me had crawled from under the bed and curiously started digging in some duffle bag laying on the floor. The bag was there because that man was a drug dealer and liked to hide his money and drugs in our house. Granny of course was upset over this but when you are in love, you are also blind to the dangers another's career choice could put our family in.

The scene then changes to another room, I can see the key chain I carry today on the dresser, confusion in my mind as I walk by. A lady is on the bed and another is standing in the mirror, durag on her head and tank top on her chest. It is apparent they were a couple and had just had sex moments before, the lady on the bed is watching a video of something on a laptop, from a side glance it looks a lot like the porn videos I had been watching on my computer before. The lady in the mirror is rapping her rhymes and then to my side I see there is drugs as well in a bag on the floor. Homosexuality, drugs, hip-hop, and pornography; all these things I had been chasing after for the past couple of weeks are in this room, in the bed, and on the floor. The voice of God' is now speaking to me, telling me these things I see are what he knows I do now and know are a sin yet choose to do anyways. Because of my decision I will not go to heaven but to hell. He then explains to me why, he knows all my excuses and all the doubts I had formed in my mind and proceeded to crush every one of them.

In my life, recently I had convinced myself that God must have changed and that because the bible was so old and written so long ago that it should only apply to the people then. I had told myself that in the times I live in, the people and culture are so much more advanced than the time of which God had written the rules, so they must have change and that he has different rules for us than the people in the bible. "Being gay is okay", pornography and masturbation are not that bad, and drugs were harmless fun. God however, told me he knows that I know these things are wrongs, he even shows me the very moment I learned right from wrong; I am in kindergarten, sitting in a group full of toddlers in the play area of a familiar classroom watching our morning cartoons. The characters on the screen sing their songs and tell their stories, giving morning lessons. The one we are watching is about the consequences of doing the wrong thing especially when you have been told and warned.

Children are not listening to their parents, teenagers are rebelling in schools, and adults are making choices to be of worldly fascination instead of being children of God. All these choices and actions we take in many different stages of our lives that at any time can end in the ultimate betrayal of God and the ultimate consequence. Like an old bedtime story many forget but like a nagging thought in the back of our minds we all know there is something we need to recall. On this night I had ignored that feeling too long and He would show me I knew better, and I could not dispute this nor make a case against it. He then told me that he also knew I would be counting on one fact about him to help me out of this pit I had crawled into. That of all the things I choose to ignore, that for me to remember he was a forgiving God was what a lot of his creation too loved to do in this very moment. Count on his mercy and his love to be a saving grace in our last moment, that because He forgives all, I would think my sins now too would be wiped away and my soul cleaned and made new. But then he said that he gave me so many chances to do right on earth and in every opportunity then he truly would have forgiven me too. He showed me images, clips, jokes, and even these new memes we love to share of Facebook and Instagram about what people thought hell was like. Dancing and joking around in a hot room with our friends, you and your buddy partying in hell and that it is just a hot room and hell isn't all that bad and jokes like "I take fiery showers I can handle a little heat". All these jokes about the one place he created for the worst of his creation and you think that is what hell is like,

He asks me. You think you know what pain you will feel and that you would rather burn than be obedient? He then recalls to me scripture I had once read as a child, that hell would be the most excruciating pain I would ever experience and would last all eternity and no matter my begging or pleading it would never end.

In my entire life the most excruciating pain I had ever physically felt had been on that childhood bedroom floor, scraping my shins on the edge of the bedpost. And like a finalizing stamp, a guaranteed signature, an owner's manual slammed on the table before me, he then told me that pain I felt then is nothing compare to what hell would feel like. Then like a game of "what if's" he would wager my sins and my justifications before me, my good deeds and my bad ones, my thoughts and my words, my wants, beliefs, my entire life's journey and whether the way I live would be enough to get me into heaven or condemn me to hell.

His voice was all I could focus on, maybe I still had a chance; at least I was hoping. Then I would hear, "you have sinned against me, even though you knew it was wrong, but you say you were confused and wasn't sure if it was okay now from then. You were not sure if your actions were a sin anymore, but you had been told and I know that you learned the consequences of right from wrong. You know I love you and all of those beneath created along with you and you know I am a forgiving God. You think I should forgive you and allow you into my grace, into heaven." My pulse is racing, my hopes at an all-time high, hoping and hanging on to his every word; maybe, just maybe I will get in. Everything goes to an eerily serious, in a matter of fact way, He says "I told you right from wrong and you choose wrong, you are going to hell." From my lips I attempt to blasphemy Him and then I feel the most unbelievable, unexplainable, unfathomable pain ever. There was not just one feeling of fire or flame, but every pain and torment in the world ever thought of and more. So unbearable I could only experience the pain for a moment before I black out.

Then I am back.

There is a white light over the bed, I am back in the room, but that pain is back as well. I try to wriggle and inch away from the searing pain, but my body is so weak that I can barely move. He is speaking again, telling me something but I cannot really hear, I look to my side and my they are there trying to get my attention, someone is patting my head with a cold towel. "Come on back, come back". Then tenfold, the pain is back and burning a hole into my head and all I can feel is hot and cold, black and white pain of hell. Then it fades a bit to the side, yes! Please stay there I do not want to be in pain anymore, I cannot take it I mentally exclaim. No, no, no, it is coming back, ahh! I internally scream. Then it passes to the other side of my head, like a blade of death hanging on a pendulum swing back and forth over the line of my life being held center. He then asks me if I really want to stay or should He just send me back to hell? Am I going to listen and follow his law? Yes! I answer, I do not want to go to hell. But God does not just give me my life back, does not allow me to come back to the living world of opportunity and free will, I must fight for my soul. So He places the blade into place over me, and then releases the string holding it taunt, then the hardest fight I would ever fight begins, my what ifs and maybes weighed against me before would now become my will power and strength to endure over my condemnation and whether I would give in to the pain like I had given in to the temptations of the worldly charms before.

So, I fight on as angels and demons taunt and cheer me on; through the night they would judge and condemn me, forcing me to choose whom to listen to and whom to ignore. They would make me choose my power or my pain, once again I would be given the options and the decision over my life; I wanted to live. So, the pendulum fell, slashing over my head blinding me with excruciating pain, and as it passed, I tried to get momentum against it, get out of the bed and huddle behind the dresser in the corner. I would do anything to ground myself against the oncoming blade to try to stop it from falling and scraping my soul. But my body is pulled back up onto the bed, I feel the lashes slashing at my back, and my shins against the bed post and the hot cold pain of hell. I shout, "No!" and begin to go in the other direction, I pull and drag myself from the bed again, fighting for a little edge and I get a little give and decide to get as far away as possible running out of the room and towards the front door to get away pushing and pulling away from the angels and demons in my way to get only as far as the front door when I'm stopped and all I can do is shrink into the corner by the shovels and shoes. "No, I am not going back up, let me go" I yelled, but they are grabbing and start pulling me up the stairs, my body is going to the stage and the pendulum is swinging back down, trying to pull me with, causing pain again and again, draining from me my energy and my will to keep going on. For what I can only estimate as about eight hours of fighting for my life that night, I pulled and pushed, clawed and dug in deep trying to hold on to the cliff opened over the open pit of hell waiting for me to give in.

Hours later, I am losing my strength and they are asking me if I am ready for it to be over, if I am ready to come back to God. I say yes, but they say they do not believe me, "maybe she needs to go one more time, they say". "No, I am ready", I say, "no more times", but one more they say and with all my energy spent they release the blade hanging taunt and I fight once more. I think of my mother, my sisters, my family, and even the strangers I have yet to meet that are also family too me, but most of all I think of my destiny. Why I need to stay, not just for myself, but for others who need me; those dear who really love me and those who are still unknown who also need me. The passion of my flesh that brought me to this very moment and the control it will no longer have over me. One last time I fight, with all my heart and soul I fight, and He lets me stay, returning my soul to my body, I'm given life again; another chance with all new tools to do my best and get it right this time. Nevertheless, he also tells me my days are numbered, I will die again and a lot sooner than what was meant to because of my sins now and today. He asks how long I think I should live, and my answer is forever and ever as I am too afraid of another day soon to come with pain like what I feel tonight ever to come. Instead he tells me his plans for me, and I accept what he deems for me and am happy to have what He offers me. But more than my life alone, but that of my future family and till today I get to keep my visions of what is to come for me. The most important part of why he allowed me the chance to fight, a chance he does not offer many; to help the lost youth of my city.

XI

In Milwaukee, the children I guard are so lost and ignorant to the sins they commit every day; I am stationed by God to watch over and see these things. Sins that would surely send them to hell without someone to steer them clear and bring the word of God to them; open their eyes so they too can experience his grace and mercy. I have always taken on the role of a protector; in middle school I would protect others from bullies and in my teenage years stand up to men to protect my family. I naturally have a nurturing personality, a love for children, the less fortunate, the animals, and the trees. Even when no one reciprocates my care for them, abandon and give up on me; I continue to the best of my ability to put others needs before my own. Some might say it is a hindrance, but I declare it a virtuous part of me that runs strong in the people of my family tree. Additionally, the youth of my city need more people in their lives who care and who want to guide and teach them. The youth need not only role models and "big brothers", but also better outlets than the corruption they see on TV and the raps they listen to on the daily. When you look beyond their deeds you can then see the scared children looking for anyone to not give up on them and pull them in from the streets. They are not a menace to society or monsters too far gone to be redeemed, but God's children and a product of what they see.

Their parents are stuck in poverty, lack proper education, and are directly affected every day by discrimination, community dysfunction, and genocidal assassination by the governing policies. The only fun available to them is the dirt they do in the streets. There are no longer safe after school programs, or community hangouts for them to escape to when things are not good in the hood. To some I have already told, the things they chase after are temporary and not worth it, doing right and working for something you can legally call your own will be better because only God then can take away the freedoms you have earned. Since that night I have decided to listen to God more closely, be obedient, try better to do well and prevent the wrong. My first step is continuing in my position in youth corrections, help the youth, teach the wrong from the right, to help them strive to do good; not put them in the corner and forget about them as the government has and continues to do.

Mothers, I plead of you, be the rod that corrects your child and never give up on them. No matter how old or ever changing the seasons that may come. Continue to be strong, for when you give up, the devil comes knocking to take what you decided to let go of. The devil has his darts of misdirection aimed and tipped with deception to destroy the future through the potential that could be lost when we let go and give up on the next to come. The generation that come after us are the seeds of our troubles and the reflection of the hard work we fail to do. Nevertheless, do not fear and do not fret for we are not expected to be perfect, for the Lord is an all forgiving and gracious God. However, know that if you turn away from Him, choosing not to raise your children in the way of the Lord too, you will forever be in turmoil, tormented by the sins you've committed and the knowledge that you had the choice to do good.

Know that God is all knowing of our doubts and all questions we may have of him and to every one of those questions, God had already provided the answers. I implore you to read and search for yourself as I do for the Holy Bible is not only the history of our people, but an infallible tool God has provided for you. Much like myself, God has awakened many others too, online, in literature and in music they testify too. Go and read the scriptures we add, verify that itching "what if" inside of you. Through my research I reveal to you I have come across many, listened to their testimonies and read about the messages of God breathed like fire through them. These lessons, visions, and experiences being had are not only for their benefit but for all to benefit too. Another young lady in South America, through her quest to become closer with God testified of when she was taken from the human plane and shown the torments of hell and the wonders of heaven. God even revealed to her that He'd chosen her much like many more because he wants to save all his children, give a chance to all to come back into his grace as promised, this is all he wants to do.

God has said that in today's age, so many more perish than those that come into his gates. Like sand being thrown on the beach, countless grains are like the souls that fall from earth into the fiery abyss. God weeps inconsolably and Jesus groans in pain because regardless of all their gifts to mankind; Jesus himself dying for our sins, how lost the world has become. God have mercy on our souls. All the things she saw, the people whom had fallen, the sins for which they suffered for even more so, frightening because I myself had been guilty too for so many accounts of my actions I surely would have fallen too. I quiver with utter realizations and I shake with decisive rebellion against the desires of my flesh. I know that I will struggle for many years to come with my free will and being able to correct the habits and conditioned responses I have become accustomed to. However, knowing of heaven and hell is enough God said; that once a child, no matter the age, acknowledges he does exist he or she is then accountable alone for the wages of their sins. So, I beg of you to fear the wrath of God and raise your children to do the same. For only then can you truly keep safe those you proclaim to love of it has already been told. "The Lord is not slow about His promise, as some count slowness, but is patient toward you, not wishing for any to perish but for all to come to repentance." (2 Peter 3:9 NASB)

I declare for myself that very night, I would reconnect and build a relationship again with God. For so long I had chosen not to go back to the church house; even against my family's pleas, how selfish and cruel of me. I would deny us fellowship and to be in the presence of his almighty word. Sure, the could continue to listen to his word and fellowship online, but to be without a shepherd, so long outside of the temple, away from his holy sanctuary; where the presence of the Lord shines true and the words are spoken onto you is indeed unbelievable but a choice I made that now I can undo.

Children, teens, adults, and elders open your ears, soften your hearts, and go back to the old ways; to when you were loving to all and a follower of God's word unquestioningly. Read the word and follow his law because the actions we commit or fail to can condemn not only us but the others who follow you. The young look up to and learn from what they see others do, mimicking our speech, mannerisms, and habits. Families linked in blood and families created through bond can fall one behind the other or rise like angels in the sky. Please listen and heed my words, God is real, heaven is too, the end may not be tomorrow but is ever more so near. No amount of days is guaranteed to anyone; only God knows and determines our time and the boundaries of our lives. Do not wait, do not procrastinate for your eternal soul is nothing like the shows on TV. No uploading to a cloud or afterlife cities built like a video game. The is no data banks with space for rent with more luxuries dependent on your amount of money. Join in fellowship, repent your sin I plead "for the wages of sin is death, but the free gift of God is eternal life in Christ Jesus our Lord." (Romans 6:23 NIV)

Weeks later, I am a bit anxious about my every move and afraid to make a mistake and slip back into my old ways. I read the word and search for answers, the infallible key. I throw away any ungodly possessions, delete music, and control what I watch on my television, demons are real said the Lord and they are rushing to destroy humanity. I then am rushing to build my armor because I know where I want to be; with God almighty through Jesus Christ, so I repent all my sins daily. I want my name to be written in the book of life and I want to Him to choose me, call my name in the end. However, so sad I become when I think of the fate of the world, how has humanity become so blind and instead listen to the desires of sin. Everywhere I look I see the trickery, the deceit, and the raps of thine enemy. The radio stations, television programs, literature, and movies are all promoting for us to sin. Companies advertise worldwide not the Lord but the desire of flesh, drugs, sex, and money. False prophets, adulterers, homosexuality, and the murderers grow in number by the day, what was once so shameful, now is promoted, funded, and taught to the youth of our cities. Dictionaries, textbooks, the internet; most dangerous above all, provide information created by anyone that can be distributed to everyone. So many lies and mockeries, so much redirection and selfish people, trading their souls for riches now instead of eternity in a city made of silver and gold.

I am sad for humanity, today is April 17, 2020 and the Coronavirus is in full affect across the nations. So many people are dying, and I can only wonder how many are falling instead of rising into God's hands. Then you look around, perk up your ears and all you hear is the wickedness about the world. People sing along to ungodly music, share links with upsetting videos, and join in with their darkest thoughts. People are so blind to the little things they do that condemns them; how or when did humanity go so wrong again. When did we again betray the Lord that his presence is not as strong as then? In the bible, the Lord would come down in flame and smoke, would speak directly to the masses; like thunder his voice would boom. He sent miracles and he struck down those against him, He sent the ark and the people would build temples he would visit and claim them. That we do not follow him stronger or more than we do hip-hop artist and reality television shows is so wrong; do people even know that they condemn each other more and more. "Hey, listen to this" or "watch that", online dating and quick hook ups, God condemns the fornicator and the adulterer; all sins he already foretold are equally weighted, not one less offensive for He said it is the law.

What all have I changed in my life, what have I done toward my destiny so far? For starters I have read God's from Genesis to Revelations and like a PG household if there is too much ungodly content, I remove it before it can get into my soul. Somethings I cannot take back however I repent for them all; tattoos I had etched into my skin, body modifications to bend with the trends, and fornication for my own gratification. However, my entire life has been shaken up and turned upside down. Thankfully, my family through my tribulation continue to love and accept me, how blessed am I. I thank you God and in Jesus name I surrender myself to thee. Help me to do your work and wake up whom I can; keep me safe from thine enemies.

Printed in the United States
By Bookmasters